TAKING LIBERTIES

DUNCAN FORBES

Duncan Forbes

Taking Liberties

London
ENITHARMON PRESS
1993

First published in 1993
by the Enitharmon Press
36 St George's Avenue
London N7 0HD

Distributed in Europe
by Password (Books) Ltd.
23 New Mount Street
Manchester M4 4DE

Distributed in the USA
by Dufour Editions Inc.
PO Box 449, Chester Springs
Pennsylvania 19425

© Duncan Forbes 1993

ISBN 1 870612 27 2 (paper)
ISBN 1 870612 32 9 (cloth)

The paperback edition comprises 1000 copies;
the cloth edition, limited to 25 copies,
is signed and numbered by the author.

Acknowledgements

Some of these poems have appeared, or are due to appear, in the following: *Acumen, Ambit, Aquarius, Illuminations, London Magazine, Modern Painters, Poems for Alan Hancox, Poetry Durham, Poetry Now, Poetry Review, Stained Glass Martyrs, The Author, The Observer, The Spectator, Understanding.*

The detail from Howard Hodgkin's lithograph *Black Moonlight* (1980) is reproduced by kind permission of the artist. Duncan Forbes and the Enitharmon Press wish to express their thanks to Sir Howard, and also to Lumley Cazalet Ltd for the transparency.

The text of *Taking Liberties* is set in
11pt Times by Bryan Williamson, Frome, Somerset
and printed by
Antony Rowe Ltd, Chippenham, Wiltshire.

Contents

The Way Things Are

The coffee shivers in concentric rings
And as the quayside seems to float inland
I walk on deck for sea-air and to watch
Weymouth become a postcard of itself,
Dorset a breakwater, the coastline cloud,
Our wake a ragged motorway of foam,
Where both a pigeon and a cabbage white
Are following the Red Ensign out to sea.

Back in the cafeteria-lounge, the youth
In Megadeth T-shirt and blue neckerchief,
The skull-and-crossbones buckle on his belt,
And reading Isaac Asimov is my son.
The girl with hiccups, sipping Diet Pepsi
And wearing a pink T-shirt, is my daughter.
Black cut-off jeans, blue watch-strap, pony-tail,
She's playing Guns N' Roses on a Walkman.

Rock muzak, rucksacks, Keep This Ship Tidy Bins,
Bermuda shorts, a Michael Jackson T-shirt,
A girl with ear-rings eating custard creams,
The mood is holiday and duty-free.
My wife is reading a Virago novel,
The Way Things Are by E. M. Delafield.
She's chewing Orbit sugar-free chewing-gum
But says she'd love 200 cigarettes.

Safety announcements in both French and English
Have spoken of emergency procedures,
Life-jackets, muster-stations, crew and drill,
A series of short blasts upon the whistle,
While I imagine what would happen if,
And in the daydream minutes before drowning
I play the hero and apologist
For love so long denied and ill-expressed.

Recension Day

Unburn the boat, rebuild the bridge,
Reconsecrate the sacrilege,
Unspill the milk, decry the tears,
Turn back the clock, relive the years,
Replace the smoke inside the fire,
Unite fulfilment with desire,
Undo the done, gainsay the said,
Revitalise the buried dead,
Revoke the penalty and clause,
Reconstitute unwritten laws,
Repair the heart, untie the tongue,
Change faithless old to hopeful young,
Inure the body to disease
And help me to forget you please.

Uley House

The flattened molehills stepping-stone the lawn
Towards fresh soil-heaps near the Judas tree.
Pink clematis flowers embrace a rusty cypress.
The creaking wingbeats of a wood pigeon
Applaud its exit from a copper beech
Into a sky of Pentecostal light
On a jasmine, bluebell, lilac-scented evening.
Rooks argue and a dog barks at a gunshot.
Among full moons of dandelion clocks
Heifers are tearing grasses in the sunset.
It's country life as *Country Life* would have it
And I'm so passive or dispassionate
I hear a desiccated holly leaf
Detach itself and fall through leaves to earth.

Red Rooms, Blue Trees

As I acclimatise
To the red rooms and blue trees,
They challenge me to take the risk
Of asking paints and canvases
Only to please and please advise.

Mandarin and clematis.
A fresco of pyjama stripes
Autographed Henri Matisse.
A forest and an odalisque
In prismatic arabesques.

A nudist in a studio,
Light-years from the Thought Police,
Lolls in an armchair paradise
Looking at goldfish in a bowl,
Hypnosis in her eastern eyes.

Bois Joly

Dog barking
on a distant farm,
sun setting,
half a risen moon,
a combine harvester's
red drone,
stubble smell,
smell of corn.

Swifts wheel above
a sunflower field,
the buds turned west,
flowers east,
where I stand like
a pantheist,
blessing sunlight,
being blessed.

12th July
'89,
Bois Joly
was the hamlet's name.
Someone else
some other time
had felt like me
if not the same.

New Year Song

Everything and nothing is
The Key to all Mythologies.
Forget the practice and the theories,
Fibonacci and his series,
Forget the sorrows of what if,
And let tomorrow come and live
With neither grievances nor grief.
Forget your hatred of surprise
And celebrate, extemporise.

A garden of exciting treats
Where sugared almonds grow on trees
With 30-carat golden sun
And hall-marked numismatic moon
May still be good enough for some
But what are they to real delights?
Become your alter egotist
Give it the slip and non-exist
Within the most enchanting tune.

Let time play truant for today,
Send hours and calendars away,
Put the starlight in a purse
And pack away the universe.
A feather on the breath of God
Who can't be known and won't be conned,
He who hears is she who listens
To the silence and the distance,
Horizons and what lies beyond.

Like expiry though with breath,
Like bereavement without death,
A passport to a Paradise
Of aphrodisiac release
With easy come and easy go
So different from synthetic bliss,
The self-disguising alibis
Of alcohol and cannabis,
Though how unknowing can we know?

Gladioli in the Vendée

My back to the afternoon sun in late July,
A man of forty, almost forty-one,
On holiday imagining I am
Vincent van Gogh or Paul Cézanne again,
I try to paint a field of gladioli.

A blue sky and a lane of flickering aspens,
The road-sign and a wall reflect the sunlight.
A glade of brushstrokes improvises leaf-blades
Where gladioli have been left to bloom
In pink, vermilion and a green-veined white.

Next day, the painting seems less numinous.
We make a detour in the car to find
The gladioli flattened, all cut down,
A slaughtered army, standard-bearers dead,
The colours darkening like closed butterflies.

There on the other side, though, of the side-road,
As if it were their liberated soul,
Pink as a flower by the asparagus,
A hoopoe stands, erectile crest erect,
A new beatitude and epiphany.

Gironde July

The wide and mud-brown tidal estuary
Was like the Mississippi, we imagined,
The ferry and its concrete landing-stage
A scene from the 1950s, we agreed,
Though river-crossing and the car-ferry
Already seem more than an hour behind.

It's 90 or a 100 in the shade;
The air outside's an oven like the car.
Dry ditches yellow with marsh marigolds
Go flickering by like vines and sunflower fields,
Though I am looking only for a bar
Which sells cold lager and iced lemonade.

We park behind a large Hôtel de Ville
Where providentially in a stone wall
We find a faucet labelled *eau potable*.
A push-button supplies it by the litre,
Splashes the feet and wets a ragged circle,
Flooding hands cupped to mouth with cold, clean water.

Meanwhile the tolling of a tinny bell
Is summoning to some ceremonial
The middle-aged of this provincial town,
All carrying their jackets for the heat.
A festival or saint's day? We can't tell,
Although there must be much to celebrate

Or so I think as we drive past the road-sign
And Mortagne, Mortagne-sur-Gironde,
Becomes a place to which I must return
If not in person sometime then in mind
As if the answer could again be found
In water reminiscent in the sun.

Wanted

'Is there a word which means
deliberate omission?'
And yes the Latin *praeteritio*
surfaces from over twenty years
and twenty centuries ago,
which is another form of preterition,
this forgetting what we know.

'Did you wear flares
or long hair as a student?'
Wanted: pictures of yourself when young
for routine mockery by
another generation.

We search the albums
for psychedelic kipper ties,
platform heels and bell bottoms,
and find instead
among pram babies now eighteen
the long unfashionable parade
of smiling and of anxious dead.

There's Jane's wedding near Leeds
with you and your friend
as Victorian bridesmaids
in striped dresses and straw boaters,
Jane who died before she was forty,
your father likewise dying of cancer,
my mother in her invalid phase,
while all the children seem so young
and we ourselves no more than children.

So we choose this black and white one
from a wedding a year before our own.
It's 1968, the year of Prague,
Jan Palach and the Evènements.
Champagne-drunk in a Devon garden,
you wear my hired grey tophat,
I your boater at a jaunty angle.
We both look young and foolish enough
to be sempiternally in love,
while over twenty years since then
are preterite, have come and gone
into our memories and oblivion.

On Such a Night

We crossed the water by a duckboard bridge
A fraction above the river's darkened surface
And lay flat on our backs there on the beach.

Sand particles in our hair and stars above us,
Spectators of the galaxy we're part of,
We glimpsed the instant of a shooting star,

And touching on infinity and each other
I would have held your hand if such a séance
Could have redeemed ourselves and life together.

Instead we followed the shoreline past plantations
Of folded beach umbrellas in the sand,
Past seafood smells of sea and restaurant,

Towards the town, or where we thought the town was,
By walls and concrete blocks still hot to touch
As if the warmth could not escape till nightfall.

We heard the sea's night-noises feel for land,
Small waves collapsing into crevices
And interrupting fluent lights on water,

Till there it was: a place called Belvedere
Which I remember now for what it felt like
To be restored to what both feared forgotten.

Snail on an Acanthus

Suspended in a slice of air
And looking headfirst down the cliff,

A snail on an acanthus leaf
Searches for things to do or eat.

Its wrinkled footsole licks the edge.
The horns detect no thoroughfare,

So round it turns at snail speed
And helmets through the spiny glade,

All of my squiggles on the page
Mocked by a silver signature.

Heron

'Who would choose to be a heron
Wading tiptoe through the shallows,
Staring at the ebbing water,
A daddy-long-legs of a bird
Stabbing minnows for his dinner,
Flapping off on heron's errands,
Anorexic and absurd?'

'Who would choose to be a human,
Glibly, gloomily assuming
What it is to be a heron?
You who cannot even fly
Desecrate my estuary
With your sewage, oil and shipping.
Frankly, I would rather die.'

Butterfly Bush

Pursuing a scent molecular on the wind
Towards mauve perfumes and a nectar feast,
Red Admiral, Peacock, Brimstone, Tortoiseshell
Are lured towards intoxicating liquor.
With pedal power in flight and puppet landing,
A Cabbage White is waltzing with its shadow.
A flake of sky-blue sky floats down to earth.
A bronze-eyed leaf, each eye with eyeshadow,
When frightened by a bear-like bumble bee,
Opens and shuts pretending to be cobra.
Shantung, Byzantine, prehistoric jewels,
Their names already metaphorical,
Feed, flirt and sunbathe on the buddleia
As if July and daylight cancelled winter.

Nil Return

Ask the present
to present
whatever isn't
an event

Ask prehistory
to deny
the ancestry
of night and day

Ask the future
to foretell
how a failure
cannot fail

What's the question
or the quest?
Let the Christian
answer Christ.

Annotating
nothingness
values nothing
more or less.

Speculation

Look in the mirror
And what do you see?
Not an admirer
In facsimile
But the cold stare
Of a grey sea.

Look at the window
And what do you see through
Beside the standing
Portrait of you?
Not your surroundings,
Nor a sea-view,

But a dying star
Warming the water,
Without a creature
Or creator.
Enter the dark
Before and after.

Sometimes

Sometimes I think what I would miss by dying
And I become the sentimentalist
Who loves both sound and smell of bacon frying,
The feel of children's hair on heads I've kissed,
Blue Malverns in the distance on the skyline
Collecting moons like a numismatist.
So is the self so unself-satisfying
It hopes life after death may not exist?

What Next?

Picture a planet
ploughing a furrow
from yesterday
towards tomorrow

Imagine life
and people on it
imagining space
as infinite

Imagine death
and what's beyond it
as both the end
and open-ended

as if the River
Universe
were both forever
and a hearse

and what you've got
is what you have
from the high-chair
to the grave

as if the night
beyond the tomb
were also that
before the womb.

Keepsakes

The two-faced cardboard parrot could kill houseflies
But not those pedalling on the yellow gumstrip.
The milk-jug wore a lace-cap fringed with beads
The colours of stained glass and medicine bottles.
A wind-up gramophone carved like a pulpit
Sang Caruso and then *Ol' Man River.*
The Shepherd Boy asleep on a sunlit chalkhill
Held all of boyhood to a day in August.
Opaque monocles of honesty rattled in the garden.
Sticklebacks and minnows from the watercress river
Were fed with breadcrumbs and died in jamjars
In the apple-green kitchen where our Granny Nona
Had seen an angel and annoyed my father.

Political Prisoner

Up to my feathered neck inside the cavern
Of your intestines, I devour the protein
Which grows again like tapestry or mould.
The entrance to the wound is never healed.
The rock-points fester in your shoulderblades,
The crag both crucifix and precipice,
A Calvary of alpine solitude.
With beak-like talons and a claw-like beak,
Your uninvited guest, I perch and feast
Upon your innards like a liver-fluke.
The manacles and fetters flinch with pain,
Which, heated by the sunlight like the granite,
Craves all day long earth's shadow known as night,
The great moth-eaten blanket of the sky,
Till frostbite also binds you hand and foot,
As haloed moons diminish to ripped toenails.
What would you dream of if you fell asleep
In the Grand Canyons of your moonlit mind?
Philanthropy again and fire on earth?
Or sun-stroke, dew-thirst, glaciers, blindness, snow?
You dread my shape heraldic on your skyline,
A Bronze Age bird and your avenging angel
Staining the sunrise and its mandala.
What would you choose now if you still could choose?
Life everlasting or tyrannicide?

Customers

The sky's in purdah.
Two dead shuttlecocks
perch on a dusty windowledge.
The ropes and nets in the gymnasium
are tied back like girls' hair.
Eleven candidates
are sitting *Use of German*
Indian file between
93 empty chairs
at 94 empty desks.
4.30 on a Friday afternoon.
And how would you express
the following in German?
That's the way to treat customers.
I'd like six strong nails.
A tube of all-purpose adhesive.
The sky's in purdah.
Two dead shuttlecocks.

Prisoner of Conscience

Thirteen shiny tins
of John West Pink salmon
have been spot-welded, I think,
onto a curved steel wire
to simulate body and spine
of a sockeye salmon leaping
out of the sculptor's mind
into the leasehold air
of a shrine to art and Mammon.

Fish-head and fish-tail
are burnished aluminium.
The eyes of Indian ink
follow you round the room.
If salmon could speak to salmon,
this creature would be
their crucified Statue of Liberty.
By the millennium
perhaps it will stink.

Double Take

A mirror hung at head-height
with a mere two words, WET PAINT,
written in capital letters
in juicy red acrylic
across the lower glass,
queries the nature and point
of life, identity, art,
the paint being no longer wet –
relative truth and all that.

So turn the eyes eyes-right
from their doubles in the glass
and read the unframed white lies
printed in black on card:
Self Portrait (Unfinished)
Artist: Sue Dominy
at can it be? Look twice.
£5,000,000.
Caption: 'We all have our price.'

Private View

The shattered mirror
on the wall
is glued together,
mosaic-style.

The melodramatic
drops of red
are real symbolic
wine or blood.

Look at the ego's
shattered egghead.
Read the bogus
suicide note.

It's a two-way mirror
after all.
The clairvoyeur
dislikes your smile.

Mirror-image
sky on water
scorns, as mirage,
glue and glitter.

Not Tested on Animals

Dear Andrew & Barbie, Many thanks.
Moroccan Rhassoul Mud Shampoo
For Hair Type: greasy with dry scalp!
How could you and how did you know?
A Body Shop shampoo which leaves
Moroccan grit grains in the bath
And looks like genuine sham poo.
Oh thank you, thank you, thank you both
And Happy New Hair to you too!

Story of My Life

Trying to free
like a good Hindu
a bumble bee
from the garden shed
I drove it into
a spider's web,
alas, instead.

There trussed and trapped,
a stumbling thing,
it buzzed and flapped,
from angry bull
with grey-haired wing
to irritable
fungus ball.

I flicked it outside
on the tip of a trowel
into the weeds
of a flowerbed
to disentangle
self from web
or try to try to try till dead.

Mr Larkin

'This was Mr Larkin's style. It stayed
Consistent all his time with Faber, till
They lost him.' Disappointments, hopes that fade,
Pair up with minor failures of the will

To undeceive a gloomy poet chap,
Ironic, doubtful. 'Mr Larkin put
Contemporary verse back on the map.'
Death, boredom, fear and the iambic foot,

No trace of passion, violence or myth –
'I'll use it.' So it happens that I write
As Mr Larkin wrote, and tinker with
The same wry neo-Georgian stuff, and fight

By shrugging it all off as passing fad
The moderns A. Alvarez plugs as greats.
I know my Larkin: what he liked of trad.,
His preference for Hardy over Yeats,

Why he kept plodding on with form and rhyme –
Likewise his critic chums: Anthony Thwaite
Who praised him on the radio all the time,
And Amis who was quick to call him great.

But if he saw artistic suicide
Pre-empting the death to which his poems led,
And told himself that such was life, and sighed
And grumbled, without casting off the dread

That what we write defines our inner nature,
And at his age having no more to show
Than two good books should make him almost sure
He could have written better, who's to know?

(1977)

Obiter Dicta 1, 2, 3

1

Christ and Buddha
Wrote no books,
Nor did Socrates.
So why put pen to paper,
Why word-process trees
If not for William Shakespeare,
If not for *War and Peace*?

2

Minor novelist, lesser poet,
We scribblers annotate the planet
As if each pebble had a call
For egotistical banal.

Sub specie aeternitatis
Who would choose to be an artist
Except the idiotic Id
Deluded into playing God?

3

O substantive for which there is no substance,
Creator and creation of the mind,
Allow me the belief in without end
To add one perfect cadence to the world.

Thinks Bubble

Instead of idling in the sun
This sunny Sunday afternoon,
The local ladybird population
Seems heaven-bent on copulation.
Dot-to-dot and tail-to-tail,
Female under thrusting male,
On sticks and stones or lumps of earth
Without restraint or thoughts of birth,
Vast herds of ladybirds are flocking
For ultra-fricative interlocking.
It's April Fool's Day. Just my luck
That you're not here to share the fun.

Personal

Law-abiding citizen
Domesticated male
Seeks a Miss Adventure,
Seeks a bit of tail.

Purist puritanical
Perfectionist and prude
Wants pornographic pleasures
With a real pneumatic nude.

In rising Peter Panic
Boring Dorian Gray
Longs to get his end in
Before the end of play.

Quiet and non-smoking
Sober Honest Joe
Seeks volcanic Judy
With red-hot lava flow.

Mortgaged married father
Willing to be conned
Craves alcoholic frolics
With horny hot-lipped blonde.

A Level Examiner
Tired of marking scripts
Yearns to try his stamina
With secretary who strips.

Raunchy former porno-queen
Desires her Holy Grail:
Law-abiding citizen
Domesticated male.

The Rougher Sex

Deskbound despot
ossified in office
seeks young sexpot
to share fat profits.

Ironist, sophist,
outsize ego,
yearns for sybarite
with huge libido.

Shore-based mariner
seeks girl lodger,
shipshape stunner,
to jolly roger.

Hen-pecked physicist,
sex-starved egghead,
craves Headmistress
chained to bedhead.

Randy doctor
wants to rehearse
tricky operation.
Needs night nurse.

Manic-depressive
horny devil
needs a nympho –
midnight revel.

Cuckolded husband
seeks revenge.
Would-be adulterers
meet Stonehenge.

Will You?

I'd like to frisk your golden fleece,
I'd like to be your Thought Police.
I'd like to beat around your bush,
To walk across your Hindu Kush,
I'd like to anchor in your creek,
I'd like to every day this week,
To wine and dine, entice and goose you,
To be seduced by and seduce you.
You're such a gem, a brick, a treat,
A three-course meal I'd like to eat.
I like your choice of face and limbs,
Your clothes, your make-up and your whims,
Your eyes, your lips, your ears, your nose,
How could I fail to fall for those?
I'd like to lead you in temptation,
To satisfaction from sensation.
I want to lead you up the garden,
Discover which bits of you harden,
Which other parts go moist and soften,
Find out once, then show you often:
An eager beaver, horny hands,
A forest fire of urgent glands,
Nirvana now and earthly bliss,
Glans penis and Mons Veneris!
But if this catalogue of desire
Is not the courtship you require
Because seditious and audacious,
As under-subtle as salacious,
What have I got to do or say
To render you an easy lay?
Or are you really as hard to get
As a hard-on on a suffragette?

Won't You . . . ?

I'll tell you once and tell you straight,
I've no desire to be your mate.
Your sexist, sex-starved words of lust
Fill me with wearisome disgust.
As for the bit between your legs,
The phantom limb with hairy eggs,
I can quite easily resist
That over-eager egotist
Which, fuelled by decades of frustration,
Has got ideas above its station.
He-men, semen, ties and socks,
You men are all so orthodox:
See something concave or convex
And your male hormones scream for sex,
For while I like one now and then
I have no pressing need of men,
All mouth and trousers, little boys,
Displaying such transparent ploys,
So low in tact and intellect
They give no pleasure to reject.
I like male egos when deflated,
Their declarations if unstated.
I'm not a meal nor would I feed
Your seedy appetites and greed,
You beansprout in the human zoo.
My *cordon bleu* is not for you.
So, Tomcat, kindly spray elsewhere;
I'm not the one for this affair.
Need I say more? Or are you thick,
Blind, deaf and dumb like your wet wick?
How could a worm in a rubber glove
Make anything resembling love?

This Thing of Darkness

Carnal love and sexual passion
In the grip of an obsession
Cannot shake in any fashion
The hypnosis of possession
Or the mutual aggression
Of carnal love and sexual passion.

Cunnilingus and fellation,
Erotic tongue and tunnel vision
Bend the mind to copulation
In a bestial position,
Tune the brain to masturbation,
Cunnilingus and fellation.

Actual and imagined names,
Beggars cannot choose their crumbs,
Of naked mothers, schoolgirls, dames,
Parade before the pulse's drums
Enacting dreams of bedroom crimes
Until the fickle fluid comes.

And what is love if not a creed
Of mutual admiration, need?
What is lust if not the deed
Of desperate desire and greed
Of menstrual blood for manly seed
Where homicidal visions breed?

Crossing the Border

There was no border and no guard.
There is no one side or the other.
Trees, deciduous or coniferous,
Choose according to their species.
Where the frontier-posts had been
With watchtowers, land-mines and barbed wire,
A river-bed of no-man's-land
Reverted to a field of wildflowers.
There were potholes in the village roads,
Chicken and ducks. It was Saturday.
You stopped a man on a bicycle,
Asked for directions and in reply
He spoke the language fluently,
As you speak mine in a countryside
Seen from a distance most of childhood
As mountain landscape on the skyline,
Known but rarely visited till now.

We turned off down an unsigned side-road
Of stone chips by a railway line
Where we left the car with one door open
And crossed the rails as if they marked a border.
We watched a hawk there in a field with crows
Gleaning the corn left over from the harvest.
They flew as we appeared on their horizon,
The buzzard slowly flapping out of danger,
As in the prison of a long embrace,
By taking liberties, we lost our freedom.

Underpass

There is a tunnel leading to Heathrow
Which for pedestrians is a kind of hell.
I would not wish on foreigner or female
The journey down or back along that hole.

Beside a noisy four-lane motorway
The footpath leads for half a lonely mile
Towards a small low-wattage bulb of daylight.
Graffiti. Dirt. Exhaust fumes. Diesel fuel.

The heart-beat is a bird stuck in an oil-slick
But there's no other way except this ill-lit
Bleak corridor next to the cycle-track,
The air monoxide and polluted concrete.

And there's your shadow lurking with a flick-knife.
If days resembled fiction or a film,
This tunnel's where I would be mugged or murdered.
'Your passport and your wallet or your life!'

It's less than true that what we fear is fear.
We're frightened of our cowardice and the truth:
That there are earthbound souls who never soar
And want revenges for their mis-spent youth.

A History of It

Wash your hands, self-conscious Pilate,
 Steady as you shave.
The rabble clamours for Barabbas,
 Robber, vermin, slave.
The god-child deified as Jesus
 Has all mankind to save.

If Leonardo fancies Lisa,
 Let them misbehave.
Aphrodite on a sea-shell
 Surf-rides on a wave.
Galileo, Christ and Moses
 Are as equals in the grave.

Karl Marx is in the library
 Where murdered millions died
And Sigmund Freud has analysed
 Herr Hitler's Jewish bride,
While Joseph acts the gentleman
 From genesis to genocide.

Birch

The charcoal rook
is a cancerous growth
in the blackened lung
of the winter birch,

an old lady
with Alzheimer's,
seventy, eighty,
unlearning the years.

The family silver
of bark and branches
is tarnished dark
and in need of a clean.

Bald and naked,
she has forgotten
the midsummer language
of green and leaves.

Sunsets electrify
her nervous system.
Storms mime grief
in a tragic display.

With a thirsty pain
under the earth,
her identical twin
seeks water, spring.

Focus

Steady the hand to concentrate the sunbeams.
Remember pinnacles of light on paper,
The tiny smoke signal, then carbon circle,
The brittle hay-blade smoking until felled?

Or in the hands of the less scrupulous
How sunlight could both persecute an insect
Or singe the bare legs of an enemy
And flatten cities into mute surrender?

Memorandum for the Grand Panjandrum

Administrivia are more and more a matter
Of total imbuggerance to me as an enemy
Of futile form-filling and carcinogenic jargon.
Who gives an acronym for idiotic idiom,
The turgid verbiage of oligarch's dittography,
The upstart footnote and its vermiform appendix,
Minutes of minutiae, quandaries of questionnaires,
Pleonastic paperwork, labyrinths of legalese
And photocopulation? Are you a fellow-sufferer
In post-potato Europe of pre-proforma trauma?
It's the Year of the Friend and I'm looking for a pen-friend.

China Clay

I was a Betjemaniac,
I wore a Larkin smile,
My writing-desk was Audenesque
Till Yeats became my style.

My Enemies of Promise
Were Eliot and Pound.
Both Dylans, Bob and Thomas,
Beguiled me with their sound.

For dryness I chose Empson,
Though later I accuse
An overdose of verbojuice
From Heaney, Plath and Hughes.

A latter-day Catullus,
Miss Dickinson and Frost,
A fake Blake and a mystic,
I wrestled God and lost

As if a choice could influence
Derivatives of me,
The young Matisse of Plymouth
Where the river milks the sea.

Mysterium

There's Bluebeard in his château,
He licks his carving-knife,
Then eats Black Forest gâteau
Cut from his seventh wife.
The Three Blind Mice are squeaking,
'We monkeys never lie:
The Three Wise Men are seeking
A Christ to crucify.'

The wolf that suckled Remus
And his blood-brother Cain
Is hounded to extinction
By Franco's troops in Spain.
The blinded Polyphemus
Meets Samson on the street.
He's curled up like a foetus
Admitting self-defeat.

His photogenic beef-cake
Was once a sacred cow,
But Tarzan has marasmus
In his second childhood now,
And Botticelli's Venus,
The goddess of striptease,
Has Huntingdon's chorea
Or Parkinson's disease.

Medusa in a café
Is photographed by Karsh.
A cappuccino coffee
Lends her a false moustache.
Achilles and Patroclus,
Homeric lookalikes,
Kneel before the engines
Of their Harley motorbikes.

Snow White and Pinocchio,
Red Riding and Robin Hood
Play hopscotch through a minefield
In a prehistoric wood,
While Minotaurs and Harpies
Are fighting tribal wars
Where dragons' teeth are growing
And every tree has claws.

Avoidance

To counteract the outer darkness,
Inter-stellar, asteroid,
Construct a world of human weakness
To be endured, to be enjoyed.

And if the task itself seems thankless,
Improvised and anthropoid,
A formula for inner blankness
Ostensibly informs the void.

If

I think it would be jollier
Without the melancholia.

And life would mostly be a picnic
If I had never learnt to nit-pick.

Nor would I suffer jealousy
If I were you as well as me.

I want another *alter ego*
Who's neither Vegan nor a Virgo.

If irked by other loners less
I could befriend my loneliness.

If action cured all introversion
I'd be a hyperactive person.

Self-pity enervates us Britons
Existing on a lonely pittance.

I blame myself, though, not the climate
That I am not a happy primate.

Cat Pepper War

I'd like to slap a writ upon
The cat that parked its situpon
Then sat and shat a pat upon
My daffodils and flattened them
Like date-palms lying shattered on
An atoll struck by atom bomb.

The dung has such a pungent smell
I know the perpetrator well:
Our neighbour's furtive Tortoiseshell.
I'll teach that brute to wipe her arse
On any of my blades of grass.
She'd better shift her features fast.

Cat pepper war! Drugged Kit-e-Kat!
Her days will be a living hell.
I'll make a scapegoat of that cat
And flay her for a welcome mat
Then nail her dead head in the hall:
The Bitch Bulb-basher of Bengal.

On second thoughts, or rather third,
I wonder what Herr Doktor Freud
Would think I'm trying to avoid,
Like Perseus mirroring the Gorgon,
By over-reacting to a turd,
A pussy and a yellow organ.

Pen-Von-Las

In the telephone wires
Wind is intoning
A warped whale music.
Smoke from coal fires
Frays horizontal.
Gale-force westerlies
Blow out the pilots
In geyser and night-sky.

With spray and a hiss
Water is seething
Around a wet rock
As at its genesis
In the Pre-Cambrian
Igneous ocean.
No wonder Celts called this
The End of the Earth.

Curriculum Vitae

Spermatozoon, the doctor's son,
Away in a foetus, asleep in a cot,
Deformative years in a deformatory,
Classroom, pitches, chapel, dormitory,
Classicist (lapsed), non-practising Scot,
Agnostic confirmed dishonest to God,
Late adolescence, effect and cause,
Chicken to egotist, artist to id,
Marriage, mortgage and male menopause,
Pandora and box, libido and lid,
Who wants to be – put up your hand –
A fish in a gigantic pond
Known internationally and/or beyond?
Send me a postcard from Gondwanaland.

In the Underworld

Clockwatchers stare at advertising space
Where Pornutopia meets with paradise
And promised lands of vines and lingerie
Ransom their happiness at purchase price.

There is a beggar man at Waterloo,
At Piccadilly needles and syringe.
At Oxford Circus a fly-posted booth
Is advertising what the flesh will do.

The poster of a famous opera star
Has pupils made of tooth-marked chewing-gum
Which blinds his eyes and Frankensteins his stare.
A smear of curry sauce has smudged him dumb.

With his guitar-case for a begging-bowl
A student haunts a subterranean song.
A carborundum spark of stainless steel
Lights up the tunnel like a smoker's lung.

This is both human sewer and London Zoo.
Each mica grain inside its metal stair
Glitters as steely as a distant star.
We are the souls in Purgatorio.

Blurb

Here's a picture of me in a po-faced pose,
A well-groomed self looking down his nose
At all the publicity-conscious prose.

But what if he's hoping that words might matter
Above all the chances to witter and flatter?
Head of dead poet brought in on a platter.

Metaquizic

oracle
sperm
answer
womb
rhetorical
pram
question
prime
miracle
tomb
love
empirical
worm
proof

Anima

Weighing the evidence
For and against,
I hedged my bets,
Sat on the fence.

The pat and trite
Or cut and dried,
My stock-in-trade,
Was patented

Until it met
What I denied
The warmly wet
And soft inside

Where now the strange
secretions are
sticky   deranged
uncouth   bizarre

doxologies
of pollen grains
intoxicating
voice and veins.

Alpha and Omega

Start with a starfish or the sea urchins,
Smells of wet bracken, seaweed and the sea.
Swallows and Amazons near Douarnenez,
Life-jacketed children from the sailing school
Seem to fake Chinese junk fights in the bay
In dinghies with clipped sails called *Optimistes*.

Sea-mist becomes light drizzle on the pines
Above the cliff-top and the cemetery
Where gladioli and begonias
Wreathe lettered tombstones, and wrought-iron Christs
Stand on the row on row of shipwrecked masts.
End with the starlight on the crown of thorns.